Don't Turn Me Off, Lord

Other Books by Carl F. Burke

GOD IS BEAUTIFUL, MAN
GOD IS FOR REAL, MAN
TREAT ME COOL, LORD

Don't Turn Me Off, Lord

and other Jail House Meditations

CARL F. BURKE
CHAPLAIN, ERIE COUNTY JAIL
BUFFALO, NEW YORK

ASSOCIATION PRESS / NEW YORK

Don't Turn Me Off, Lord

International Standard Book Number
    Hardbound: 0-8096-1832-X
    Paperback: 0-8096-1834-6

Library of Congress Catalog Card Number: 72-167885

PRINTED IN THE UNITED STATES OF AMERICA

Dedicated to
LLOYD S. BURNS
DOROTHY F. BURNS

CONTENTS

FROM THE OLD TESTAMENT

STORIES OF QUIET WISDOM

FROM THE NEW TESTAMENT

WHAT IT'S ALL ABOUT

The physical needs of people who are incarcerated are similar to those of people who enjoy complete freedom. The needs are for food, clothing, shelter. When one is placed behind bars, his emotional needs differ in degree only from those of people on the other side of the bars. There is need for acceptance, for companionship, for security, for the feeling of being a person.

What is true of the physical and psychological needs of the incarcerated person is also true of his spiritual needs. They, too, are intensified by his present situation. Within every person, even though he may not be the least bit aware of it, there is a restless search for self-understanding and self-acceptance. The environmental, educational and family pressures; the influence of the peer group; the effects of mental and physical health are all factors in determining the direction in which the person may go in this unrecognized search for his self.

A jail chaplain frequently encounters this search moving in the direction of a rebellion which reveals itself in antisocial behavior ranging from murder to simple acts of vandalism. It shows itself in cynicism and in rejection of the chaplain and of his religious values. And, indeed, the total value system of society. A common direction, particularly among younger children, is apathy. Its most frequent symptom is that of the school dropout who "just doesn't care". It is a youth who sees no meaning in life because he, or she, has not been able to establish any meaningful relationship with members of the family, or with schoolmates, or with church groups. Obviously, there are other words which could be applied to this list—discouragement, hopelessness, paranoia, despair and other technical terms used by the psychologist and the psychoanalyst and the social worker.

Beneath it all, however, there is a spark. And to fan that spark into life represents the search, the hope, and the opportunity of the chaplain. It has been the one objective of the meditations collected here to fan that spark, and to produce conversation between the chaplain and the individual. They are not an end in themselves but a springboard to the establishment of rapport and conversation. And so they draw on a wide range of simple yet dramatic material, from common folk tales, to incidents from the biographies of famous men, to a straightforward retelling of the story of some biblical hero of the faith.

In this sense, they arise out of the special

DON'T TURN ME OFF, LORD

needs of the prison situation. And they seek to communicate in terms and language and thought patterns that have meaning and are understood by those in the chapel, without seeming so alien to the normal speech patterns of the chaplain that they simply increase the suspicion of "phoniness" in which he is already held.

I am encouraged to hope, however, that these meditations may also meet the needs and interests of a wider audience. For the special needs of the prison situation are simply the general needs of the human situation writ large. The search for self concerns us all, and frequently leads all of us down paths of rebellion, indifference, and discouragement. All of us respond to a familiar truth expressed in fresh and telling fashion.

The material presented here, then, makes no claim to originality. Some of it will be recognized as having come from other sources. Some of it I have culled over the years in reading and in experience. But, in this form, I have found it helpful in my special work, and I have set it down here in the hope and belief that it will be of help and interest to others.

CARL F. BURKE

Tales From True-Life Stories

Don't Turn Me Off, Lord

When he comes and knocks, they will
open the door.
Luke 12:36

Did you ever hear the story of Mr. Kim? When
he was only three years old he somehow got
separated from his parents in a bus station in
the city of Pusan, Korea. His parents hunted all
over the place for him and couldn't find him.
Being only three years old, he was plenty scared.
Before long he was cold and hungry. Mr. Kim
was found by a poor man who made his living
doing odd jobs wherever he could find them. He
took pity on the little boy and took him into his
own home. While he worked at his odd jobs, the
child went begging in the streets. It was nine
years before the parents, who never gave up
looking, found him and took him home with
them. They were so grateful to the man who
had helped their little boy that they gave him
enough money to go into business for himself.

The boy grew up and became known simply
as "Mr. Kim". When he inherited a lot of money
from his parents, he decided to dedicate his life,
and money, to homeless boys in Korea. He
found them in bus stations and railroad stations; he found them begging on the streets and
stealing; he found them living in caves. At first

they turned him off. In fact, they even threatened to kill him. But he kept right at it and persuaded some of them that he was not out to use them but rather to help them. He took them to the home he had established and there he taught them how to read, to write, and to work at some trade or skill.

When the boys in this home grow up and marry they are each given a plot of ground or help to get established in a business or trade. But there is one deal made. Each one must promise to take an abandoned child into his home.

PRAYER: When it's time for me to help someone else, don't turn me off, Lord! *Amen.*

What You Looking For, Man?

Where your wealth is. . . .
Matt. 6:21

A preacher by the name of Russell H. Cornwell had a famous sermon he called, "Acres of Diamonds." He preached the sermon thousands of times all over the world. It is said that he earned several millions of dollars and then in turn used the dollars to provide education for needy men and women. The sermon had as its base an event that took place in India over a hundred years ago.

A farmer owned a very small farm which he worked with great care and lived with considerable contentment and happiness. One day, the farmer had a visitor who came and spent the night with him. They sat around a small fire talking about diamonds. The visitor said that a diamond is the most expensive thing in the world. He told the farmer that if he had a diamond as large as the end of his little finger he would have a fortune.

When the farmer went to bed that night he spent considerable time thinking about diamonds and in the process he lost a very valuable possession. It was his contentment. He was now very restless, because he had no diamonds. The next morning he decided to sell his farm and go in search of diamonds so that he could be rich. He sold his farm very cheaply and everywhere he searched he found nothing. At last his money gave out and also his hope. Then, in a fit of discouragement, he committed suicide.

The man who bought the farm was wise enough to develop what he already had. Instead of spending his time on things that he didn't have, he gave himself wholly to working his

DON'T TURN ME OFF, LORD

own farm. One day as he was working in the fields he dug up something that shone in the sunlight. He took it to the local jeweler and was told that he had discovered a diamond. He went back to work and soon he found other diamonds. He had discovered what were to become the Golomo mines, the richest diamond mines in the world. He made the discovery as you and I are most likely to make any discoveries: by working with the things that we already have.

PRAYER: When my big moment comes, Lord,
may I use it well. More than that,
may I recognize it. *Amen.*

How Are You Doing?

... a glad heart. ...
Prov. 15:13

There is a person I know to whom I never say, "how you doing?" The reason is that he will tell me and it will take him at least an hour. We all have our aches and pains and we all like to talk about them.

A very famous author, O. Henry, wrote a story about a burglar who was burglarizing a house. The burglar pointed his gun at the home owner and said, "Put up your mitts." The man put up his right hand and the burglar shouted, "Put up the other one." The man replied, "I can't do it." "Why can't you?" asked the burglar. And the man replied, "I have rheumatism in my left shoulder."

The burglar thought for a moment and then relaxed and said, "Oh, me and rheumatism is old pals." Then they got into a big rap about the various symptoms of rheumatism and what effect rainy weather has on it. And they began rapping about pills and medicines and exercises and things that people do for their rheumatism. And before long the burglar had completely forgotten that he had come to burglarize the house!

So I guess it is true that all of us have our aches and pains and we like to share them with others. I have yet to run into anyone who didn't want to get rid of his aches and pains.

One of the worst kind of aches is when we are discouraged and about to give up and it seems like nothing is going right. The best medicine I know for it is found in the Book of Proverbs. "A glad heart makes a cheerful countenance." It is good because, for one thing, it doesn't taste terrible like some medicines we have all taken. It is a good medicine to take, too, because it doesn't have any side effects. I never knew anyone who has ever been hurt by taking this medicine. Perhaps the main reason for taking it is that it works. There are thousands of sick people who would be helped back to health by cheerfulness and no doubt there are thousands who die because they refuse this medicine and they have lost heart in hope. No doubt one of the best reasons for taking this medicine is that it helps others as well.

Everyone of us have all the discouragement we need. We all come up face to face with enough gloomy people to make life difficult. If gloom is contagious, then so is cheerfulness.

PRAYER: Life is more than gloom, Jesus, we know that. But please help us to believe that. *Amen.*

Happiness Is . . .

The measure you give will be the
measure you get.
Mark 4:24

Somewhere I read a story of a happy and busy man. As I remember it he was an old man and had been a stone mason all of his life. Shortly after he retired his wife passed away and he donated his time to a church youth camp to help build cabins and other buildings that were needed.

During the summer some of the older teen-agers had a chance to work with this man and learn how to lay bricks and mix mortar. But they also learned from him how to live.

We will call the stone mason Jim, though that may not be his name. One of the things that Jim taught the members of the youth camp was that in this crazy, mixed-up world of ours, everybody needs a little time to be alone. Time to think and to rest, and to catch up with himself. It is like a plan that was practiced by Christ, who made it a habit to be alone at times to think, to pray, to rest.

Jim also taught the young men at the camp that everybody needs to have some kind of sat-isfying work to do, the kind of work a man can look back on and feel that he has accomplished something. Perhaps that is why a good many men have a hobby in woodworking, or automo-bile mechanics, or building model trains, air-planes and racing cars. Perhaps that is why Christ himself was a carpenter.

Jim also taught his young men that they needed a set of rules to live by, a set of values that would help them face up to life. A stone mason has ways of measuring rocks and know-ing what is square and what is true. He learns what should be thrown away and what should

DON'T TURN ME OFF, LORD

be kept. He also learns that rocks and stones and bricks that are thrown away sometimes can be used again in another spot. Perhaps he even knows the truth of the saying that is found in the Bible "that what was rejected has become the chief stone."

We are all too busy and we get away from these basic needs that Jim taught his young men: the importance of being alone to rest and to think; the importance of doing something worthwhile and of having rules to live by.

PRAYER: Jesus, help us to really live, and in living to find happiness. *Amen.*

He's Got It

> Put into practice what you have learned.
> Phil. 4:9

Somewhere along the line we have all heard these words, "Listen, my children, and you shall hear of the midnight ride of Paul Revere." They come from a poem by Henry Wadsworth Longfellow. We all remember Paul Revere as a very daring horseman, riding throughout the land, calling, "The Red Coats are coming." But actually he should be remembered for much more than this. He was an outstanding American in many ways and is numbered among those whose strength of character helped mold the firm foundation upon which our country is built.

It was said of Paul Revere that he was a man of so many abilities and achievements that there will likely never be another like him. And truly it would be difficult to catalog all of his astounding achievements.

He was an engraver of great skill and his etchings of scenes and events of the time in which he lived are of great historic value. In the museums, especially in the Boston area, there are many things that he made out of silver and gold.

Yet, for all his greatness as an engraver, it is hardly known that he designed and printed the first paper money used by the government.

At the outbreak of the Revolutionary War there was only one small powder mill in all of America. In 1775, Paul Revere constructed a larger and more efficient plant and personally supervised the making of every keg of powder. Next he turned to casting cannons, first in iron and then in brass and in bronze. After the war he turned his foundry to the more peaceful pursuit of casting church bells, and some are still in existence and famous for their sweet tones.

He was even the first coroner in Boston. He later became the first charter member of a successful fire insurance company.

Paul Revere discovered, by his own patient experimenting, the jealously guarded secret of rolling copper into sheets and of drawing it into spikes and bolts and a great many other useful utensils. He thus became the father of the American copper industry.

Paul Revere carried to every Middlesex village and farm on that historic April night a voice in the darkness, a knock at the door and the word that shall echo forever. But he left a far greater heritage to you and to me through his pioneering spirit and untiring industry. Perhaps he should be remembered as a man who used life to its fullest in contributing to the common good of all of God's people.

PRAYER: Let me use my life to its fullest
for others. *Amen.*

God's World

I will lift up my eyes.
Ps. 121:1

You have been hearing a lot about ecology these days haven't you? So much so that every once in a while we think it's a brand-new idea.

Perhaps it will surprise you to learn that concern for the world and its natural resources really goes back to 1854 when a young journalist and his bride migrated from Detroit to Nebraska Territory.

The young journalist, J. Sterling Morton, soon became editor of Nebraska's only newspaper. Thus he was in a good position to spread his convictions about tree planting. It was not simply a matter of making their new homes more pleasant. Trees were actually needed for windbreaks, lumber, fuel and shade, and as it developed, as a source of income, too. Largely from Morton's efforts, that portion of Eastern Nebraska soon became a great commercial orchard section. Morton stressed the importance of trees, suggesting that they be planted to commemorate special events such as dedications, visits of notables, and as memorials.

In one of his most famous speeches he expressed his philosophy. "There is beauty in a well ordered orchard which is a joy forever. Orchards are missionaries of culture and refinement. If every farmer in Nebraska will plant out and cultivate an orchard and a flower garden, together with a few forest trees, this will become mentally and morally the best agricultural state in the Union."

DON'T TURN ME OFF, LORD

On January 4, 1872, Morton presented to the State Board of Agriculture a resolution calling for an annual tree planting day to be known as Arbor Day.

Even then Morton was alarmed at the ravaging of our forests and the "cluttering of our land." To offset this he constantly urged the planting of trees and flowers and the preservation of the·land. In another speech it is reported that he said, "The cultivation of trees and flowers is the cultivation of the good, the beautiful and the noble in man."

Morton went on to become United States Secretary of Agriculture, but he always considered the establishing of Arbor Day his crowning achievement. And thus he became the father of the ecology movement.

J. Sterling Morton was not a brilliant man, nor a gifted man, but he was a man who used his God-given talents and God-given convictions to leave this world a little better than he had found it.

PRAYER: We can all do something to make the world better. *Amen.*

Stick With It

Do not let yourselves become discouraged
and give up.
Heb. 12:3

On April 5, 1909, the temperature was 50°
below zero and blizzard winds and snow struck
hard into the faces of six men who were making their way over the ice toward the North
Pole.

They were led by a bearded and determined
explorer, slightly over 50 years old. They pushed
at top speed when conditions permitted, sleeping only three or four hours, and then they
forced themselves on in semi-darkness.

This was no fly-by-night reckless venture un-
dertaken by some daredevil. For more than 20
years Peary worked, ate, and slept, driven by
one strong desire, to discover the North Pole.

Seven times he tried it, seven times he failed.
Now he was 52, past his physical prime, hardly
young enough to brave 50 below zero blizzards.
He knew his eighth expedition would be his
last shot at the Pole. So it had to be the best
effort of his life. On September 16, 1908, his
small ship, the *Roosevelt*, only about as large
as a tugboat, reached as far as it could go into
the polar ice and the men began carrying sup-
plies across the ice to their land base 90 miles

away. By October the sun disappeared below the horizon and the long Arctic winter began. Darkness and icy cold enveloped the expedition. By December temperatures were as low as 50 to 55 below zero. Cold was not the only enemy. There was the terrible, depressing darkness.

Peary had an antidote for cold and monotony. It was work. A young geologist made a note in his log, "We are constantly occupied, we are constantly happy. The working day isn't long enough and I have never known until now the real joy of living."

On February 28, 1909, the polar dash started. Only a few could make the final assault on the Pole. So it was that Peary, Henson, and the four Eskimos pushed their way, day after day, into the bitterest cold. Finally, 37 days after they began their ultimate push to reach the Pole, they achieved the top of the world and victory, undaunted by all that raw nature could offer to impede them. Peary and his men had conquered the North Pole and the Arctic.

This adventure is an excellent example of the importance of not giving up too soon.

PRAYER: When everyone else turns back, may we try once more. *Amen.*

Father's Day

Honor your father.
Exod. 20:12

Father's Day has become almost as important as Mother's Day. All because a minister in Spokane, Washington, decided to preach a sermon on the importance of being a father, and because of a lady named Mrs. John Dowd who was listening to the sermon that Sunday in 1909. A question came into her mind "Why not a Father's Day?"

Later she made the suggestion to the minister, whose sermon had made her think of her own father. Following the death of her mother, he had become both a father and a mother to her. And she thought of it as a way of honoring him and other devoted fathers throughout the world.

With the assistance of the minister who delivered the sermon, as well as her own minister, a resolution was drawn up that called for the observance of a father's day.

Thousands of signatures were obtained by many interested and concerned people, and the third Sunday in June was set aside for the observance of Father's Day. It was not until June 18, 1916, that Father's Day achieved national significance and observance, when it was proclaimed by President Wilson, with appropriate ceremonies in Spokane, Washington.

For Mrs. Dowd that hour meant the fulfillment of her greatest ambition and her greatest happiness. Her father had lived to share that day with her. He stood beside her, strikingly handsome, humble in the realization that he had been the inspiration for a day that would never die in the hearts and minds of a nation.

PRAYER: May all of us have fathers who know how to give love and help. *Amen.*

The Flunkie

We rejoice in our troubles.
Rom. 5:3

Did you ever sing the Christmas Carol, "O Little Town of Bethlehem?" Do you know who wrote it? It was Phillips Brooks. Most people think of him as a great preacher and the author of hymns and books. But he flunked out on his first job.

He had a lot going for him, too. He was bright, and got out of college before he was twenty years old. His first job was as a school teacher. He was given a class of tough characters. They had already been through three teachers, and they were after him, too. In fact, he thought they were a bunch of kooks and told some of his friends he was thinking of getting a bullet proof vest, or whatever it was they got in those days.

At last, that class got to him, and he quit. Walked out. His boss, the school principal, told him if he failed in teaching he would fail in everything. But he didn't go for that bit.

In later years, he became the greatest teacher in his generation. Mobs of people came to hear him. They filled the church to overflowing. The people who came were rich and poor, young and old, wise and not so wise, people with problems just the same. He knew discouragement, rejection, and what it was like to have everything go wrong—that boxed-in feeling. More than that, he knew how to help people because he had been where they were.

Many men have had to face discouragement, and a feeling of being boxed in.

It is in Christian hope and love that we find strength and courage to carry on, and not let trouble turn us off.

PRAYER: Any one can turn off, O Christ. Help me not to be just anybody, but somebody that faces life with hope, strength, and courage. *Amen.*

You a Saint, Man?

I am an ambassador.
Eph. 6:20

No doubt everyone has been called a lot of different things. But did anybody ever call you a saint? In a way you are, you know.

Probably the best known saint is St. Francis of Assisi. He lived such a simple life that everybody thinks of him as their saint. Actually, he was born into a wealthy family. He was a leader of the youth in his town. Then a strange thing happened. God called him to help the poor and the lepers. And history books and encyclopedias say that he gave all that he had to feed and clothe the hungry and the naked. It is said that he loved all of life from his fellow human beings, to the sun and the moon, and all the animals. He is best known for one of the simplest and most meaningful prayers ever written, "Instruments of Thy Peace."

O Lord, our Christ, may we have thy mind and thy spirit; make us instruments of Thy peace; where there is hatred, let us sow love; where there is injury, pardon; where there is discord, union; where there is doubt, faith; where there is despair, hope; where there is darkness, light; and where there is sadness, joy. O divine Master, grant that we may not so much seek to be consoled as to console; to be understood, as to understand; to be loved, as to love; for it is in giving that we receive, it is in pardoning that we are pardoned, and it is in dying that we are born to eternal life. *Amen.*

Weird Things

But many that are first will be last,
and the last first.
Matt. 19:30

There are a lot of weird sayings in the Bible. It seems like this verse is one of them, and that it's messed up in the order of things.

That's because we think that the people who come in first always win. But they don't. Sometimes there is more honor in losing.

You have all heard of the Indianapolis 500. One of those weird things happened in the race that was run in 1912. A fellow by the name of Ralph DePalma led the race for slightly over 498 miles and it seemed like only some sort of a miracle could let someone else win the race.

Then the miracle happened. Going into the last lap, DePalma's racer quit dead. He jumped out and began pushing it down the long last mile that remained. The spectators sat silent for a moment, sort of dumbfounded, and yet in a way in awe of his courage. Then they let out a tremendous roar of approval which could be heard above the noise of the track. It was a mighty dangerous task that DePalma set for himself. The other cars were passing him at speeds of 100 miles an hour or more. But he never looked back. He just kept pushing his car.

DePalma actually made it across the finish line just before another man named Joe Dawson whizzed past. But Dawson won the race. The rules required that the winning car cross the finish line under its own power.

But DePalma won something even greater than the Indianapolis 500, though his crossing the finish line didn't count. He showed everybody that he had courage and that he never gave up. Later he came back to win the race. In every race he entered he was the crowd's favorite. People knew that even though he hadn't been first, he had really won.

PRAYER: In trying to win, don't let us get ahead of ourselves, or of you, Jesus. *Amen.*

One Guy Is Important

You must remember all the experiences through which the Lord your God has led you.
Deut. 8:2

Some of the most outstanding events of history developed because of people whose names are almost unknown. Such a person was Jamie Greenleaves, a twelve year old boy.

On August 12, 1865, he broke his hip and was admitted to a hospital in Glasgow, Scotland. A serious infection had already set in, even before his admission. Under ordinary circumstances the young man would have undoubtedly died from septic poisoning. Surgery then was such a great risk, because of the high infection rate, that setting a compound fracture often proved fatal.

It was the boy's good fortune, however, that Dr. Joseph Lister was ready with his new discovery, the result of many years of research, called antiseptic surgery. First Dr. Lister cleaned the wound with his new antiseptic solution, to kill the germs he felt sure were present. Following the operation, an antiseptic dressing was put over the wound to prevent other germs from getting in.

All this came about because of a bottle of wine. Some years earlier Louis Pasteur of France had proved that the fermentation of wine was due to microbes. If this were true, Lister theorized, perhaps the infection of tissues had a similar cause. And if wine could be kept sweet by excluding microbes, a wound could probably be kept clean in the same way. If Lister's theory was sound, his discovery would be a landmark in the history of medicine.

The antiseptic that Dr. Lister used was a carbolic acid solution, which is derived from creosote. He knew that people used creosote to clear away the smell of rotting garbage. And if creosote could get rid of the smell, it probably also could destroy the bacteria that caused the smell. And so, on that hot day over one hundred years ago, little Jamie Greenleaves' shattered and infected hip was treated by Dr. Lister in the first successful case of antiseptic surgery. And the doors were open for surgery with safety in the future.

Perhaps thinking of these words from the Old Testament, and the experience of a young boy, may help to bring purpose to your life the next time you get to feeling that only bad things happen to you.

PRAYER: May our bad luck be the start of some one else's good luck. *Amen.*

What Are You Laughing At?

A merry heart doeth good like a medicine.
Prov. 17:22

One of our country's long time favorite funny men is Jimmy Durante. He claims that the neighborhood tough guys used to make it rough for him because he had a schnozzle that could be seen two blocks away. One day his mother bought him a "Buster Brown" suit with a large flowing collar and on Sunday she made him wear it. He knew that if the gang ever saw him he was sunk.

Suddenly, he says, he caught sight of himself in the store window. "As I looked in the glass I found myself smiling and very soon I was laughing. As I was standing there, along came four or five of the gang. They stared at me trying to figure out why I wasn't running. 'Listen you,' one of them said, 'what's so funny?' 'Look,' and I pointed to the figure in the window. 'A guy dressed like a sissy with a face like a horse.' And I kept right on laughing. Soon they were laughing along with me.

"One of the boys was all for messing me up but the leader of the gang said, 'Lay off him, he's a good guy.' It dawned on me then that as long as I could laugh I was safe from the world."

From this experience Jimmy Durante has drawn the following conclusions. "All of us have schnozzles, are ridiculous in one way or another, if not in our faces then in our character, mind and habit. When we admit our schnozzles instead of defending them we begin to laugh and the world laughs with us and not at us."

PRAYER: Teach us to laugh, but never to mock out. *Amen.*

Did You Know?

Rules and Regulations

You shall. . . .
Exod. 20:3

Did you ever go down to a bus station and see a sign that listed rules and regulations? You see signs like that in schools, sometimes at the park or swimming pool and even in a jail.

Did you ever go to the movies and see a film and in it there was a stage-coach with people riding in it? And sometimes on the stage-coach there were the words "Wells-Fargo." They had rules and regulations on the stage-coach, too. Here are some of them:

1. Abstinence from liquor is requested but if you must drink, share the bottle. To do otherwise makes you appear selfish and unneighborly.

2. If ladies are present, gentlement are urged not to smoke cigars. Their odor is repugnant to the gentle sex. Chewing tobacco is permitted but spit with the wind and not against it.

3. Gentlemen must refrain from the use of rough language in the presence of ladies and children.

4. Buffalo robes are provided during cold weather. Hogging robes will not be toler-

ated and the offender will be made to ride with the driver.

5. Don't snore while sleeping or use your fellow passenger's shoulder for a pillow. He, or she, may not understand and friction may result.

6. Guns may be kept on your person for use in an emergency. Don't fire them for pleasure or shoot wild animals. It scares the horses.

7. In the event of runaway horses remain calm. Leaping from the coach in panic will leave you injured, at the mercy of the elements and hungry coyotes.

8. Forbidden topics of discussion are stagecoach robberies and Indian uprisings.

9. Gentlement guilty of unchivalrous behavior toward a lady passenger will be put off the stage. It's a long walk back. A word to the wise is sufficient.

Somebody has said that all of the laws and all rules and regulations that have been made in all of the history of the world have not yet improved on the Ten Commandments.

PRAYER: Give us courage, Jesus, to live by your rules and regulations. *Amen.*

Big Brothers

> Whenever you did this for one of these poorest brothers of mine, you did it for me.
> Matt. 25:40

Thousands of men know the meaning of these words. They are men who were once delinquent, or disadvantaged or maybe had done some time. Or they were just plain lonely kids who had a need not only for hot dogs and hamburgers and a chance to go to an occasional baseball game or maybe fishing, but also for the warmth and acceptance, understanding, and the support of a man. They were the boys who were befriended by men who called themselves Big Brothers.

Today there are over one hundred Big Brother agencies, sponsored by Protestant, Catholic, and Jewish groups.

The Big Brother idea started in 1904 when a men's club of the Central Presbyterian Church in New York City decided it would do something different to help prevent juvenile delinquency. Each club member agreed take an individual interest in just one boy who had gotten himself into trouble with the law. As the result of that seemingly small beginning, with their unique "one man, one boy," technique, the Big Brothers have worked virtual miracles to bring lost or forlorn youth back to life and living.

Big Brothers are volunteers and they come from every walk of life. They are porters and bank presidents, janitors and jet pilots, teachers and truck drivers, mechanics and merchants. They give their time to the making of better men out of boys who need help. The motto of the Big Brothers is: "No man ever stands so straight as when he stoops to help a boy."

Little Brothers, boys between the ages of 15 and 17, come to the Big Brothers on the suggestion of clergymen, schools, courts, police, probation or parole officers, social agencies, parents or relatives; and it is not unusual for a Little Brother to bring one of his friends, saying, "This kid's gettin' out of hand. I think he needs a Big Brother like I got."

Little Brothers often need friendship, love, advice and guidance. They may be in trouble with the law, they may be emotionally upset, they may be fatherless, or in a children's home, or they may just be unhappy boys in need of adult male companionship.

In one sense, Big Brothers are like life savers at the beach, saving boys from drowning or going and getting all mixed up. They are sort of like doctors too, but the transfusions which Big Brothers give are not of blood, but of hope and love. Or maybe you could call them big game hunters. But the Big Brothers' quarry is not the lion or the tiger. It's even bigger game: boys with potential for growth and greatness, boys who are lost in life's wilderness or rejection, insecurity, indifference and hostility. But most of all they are like missionaries, proving by their care that God cares, too.

PRAYER: Help us this day, O Christ, to show hope and love that others may find the way to you. *Amen.*

Can It, Man!

For this very reason, do your best.
Pet. 1:5

Just about the time the Pilgrims were landing on Plymouth Rock, two spies were running desperately, in England, for their lives and, as they said, for their country. They had a secret almost as important to England as the secret of the powerful atom is today. But this was not the plan for a weapon that they carried. It was a well guarded secret of a method for coating tin and other kinds of metal.

The process of tinning metal is no longer a secret. It is one of the largest industries in our country. More tin cans are produced each month than the United States has people. Enough steel was used in tin plating soft drink cans last year to build two Golden Gate Bridges and still have enough left over to build another bridge over a mile long.

The Romans knew the secret of tin plating. The Phoenicians mined tin ore in Cornwall on the coast of Britain over a thousand years before Christ was born. It was known to the people in Central Europe in what is now Czechoslovakia. And it was from this area that the spies from England succeeded in learning the secret.

Tin cans are made from tin plate which is neither tin nor plate. The term refers to the process by which thin sheets of iron are coated with tin to produce a can that resists rusting. By adding one metal to another, we can produce a more usable and less expensive material.

The second book of Peter talks of the importance of adding material to our lives to produce a more usable life: add goodness to your faith, to your goodness add knowledge, to knowledge self-control, to self-control endurance, to endurance godliness, to godliness brotherly love, to brotherly love, love.

PRAYER: Jesus may we be adders to life. *Amen.*

Get With It, Man!

In the full light of truth, we live in God's sight.
2 Cor. 4:2

I heard a story once about a minister who wanted to have a house way out in the country where he could go and just "get off the world" and forget all about his troubles, with no telephone to "bug" him.

He did not have enough money to buy a place. But he dreamed about it all of the time. Finally he was able to get enough money together so that he could buy a vacant lot by the shore of a small pond and begin to build a house for himself.

He did very well in building his house until it came time to hang a door. He soon discovered that it was quite a trick. If he hung it in the open position it wouldn't shut. If he hung the door shut, it wouldn't open. No matter what he did, it just wouldn't work. So he gave up in disgust and started home. On his way home he passed a house that was being built by a carpenter. And that carpenter was hanging a door! The minister thought that if he just watched the carpenter he would learn how to hang a door. Then he could do it himself. So he stopped his car, and got out and went over.

The carpenter became uneasy at someone

standing there and staring over his shoulder. So he said to the minister, "What do you want, Jack?" The minister replied by introducing himself and telling what he wanted.

The carpenter's face lit up as he said, "I've always wanted to preach a sermon to one of you ministers. I'll make a deal with you. I'll show you how to hang a door if you will let me preach a sermon to you." That seemed fair enough. Then the carpenter said, "My sermon is different from yours. It won't have any words, but it will have three points like yours do." The minister said, "A sermon without words? Who ever heard of such a thing?" The carpenter said, "You don't let us talk back to you while you are preaching a sermon and you can't talk back to me." So the deal was made and the carpenter showed the minister how to hang a door. He tried it and it worked.

Now it was time for the carpenter to preach his sermon, so he told the minister to get into his pick-up truck and they drove off down the road. After they had gone about a half mile they stopped in front of a vacant lot, got out and walked to the back of the lot. The carpenter pointed to a foundation that was in the ground and held up one finger. Here was the first point in the sermon. The minister began to wonder what he was trying to tell him. He looked at the foundation and he knew it was a good foundation that would hold the weight of a very heavy building. The sand, cement and water had all been mixed properly. Then he looked down into the cellar and discovered that somebody had been using it for a dump. There were tin cans, old automobile tires and many other articles that you find in a dump. And still that one finger was up. The first point in his sermon. And then suddenly the minister got the point.

Somebody had made a good beginning but had gone no further, and it had become filled with junk.

The carpenter did say that his sermon had three points so they got back into the pick-up truck and drove about a mile and stopped in front of a house—a beautiful house—with a picket fence around it. The lawn and shrubbery were well kept. The house had been freshly painted. It was the kind of house we would all like to build when our ship comes in.

The minister was anxious to see the inside. When the carpenter opened the door he started in; but the carpenter pulled him back and wouldn't let him in. He just pointed and held up two fingers. The second point in this sermon.

The minister looked in, you know what he

saw? Nothing, absolutely nothing. There were no walls, no electric lights, not even the wires, no stairs, not even the risers, no floors. There was just nothing there. Then the minister noticed those two fingers again and suddenly it dawned on him what the carpenter was saying.

Here was a house that was pretending to be something it was not. It was one thing on the outside and nothing on the inside. It was all show. It must have been like what the Psalmist had in mind when he referred to people who speak with a double tongue. Sometimes we say a person is two-faced. At other times we say he gives us a "snow job."

Then it came time for that third point and they stopped in front of another house. It had a picket fence around it but some of the pickets were missing. The lawn needed to be cut and it was about time that the house was painted again. When the carpenter and minister walked up under the front porch they noticed that the bell was out of order. But that didn't seem to make any difference. The carpenter just walked right in and shouted, "Honey, I'm home." His wife came out of the kitchen and gave him a great big kiss, and two dirty-faced little kids came running out of another room and grabbed their father about the leg and began jumping up and down and shouting, "Hi, Daddy."

The minister was a little embarrassed by all this show of affection and he turned away and noticed somebody had not hung up his coat and some toys were thrown around in the middle of the floor and it looked like somebody had forgotten to sweep the floor for a day or two and even a picture on the wall was a little crooked.

All the time this was going on the carpenter was holding up three fingers, the third point in his sermon. Do you get it? Here was the house that was not perfect but it was being used for the purpose for which it had been built, for someone to live in and to make of it a happy home where people cared for and loved each other.

What would you say about your life? Is it just a good beginning that has become filled with junk? Is it just a false front for others to see, or is it the real thing even though it isn't perfect, where the love of God is shared with other people? I can't answer that question, only you can. In the answering, be absolutely honest. Tell God the truth. Because he already knows.

PRAYER: Jesus, help me to see me like I am, and like I can be. *Amen.*

Peeling Potatoes

Live in such a way to cause no trouble.
1 Cor. 10:31

You certainly can't boast that there is a great future ahead of you if you learn only how to peel potatoes perfectly. I don't know of anybody who ever felt a call to peel potatoes. Instead, we look upon it as a lousy job, and laugh at jokes about it. But still it has to be done.

Where did we ever get the idea that only those who do the great big jobs are doing things that are important?

God wants all men to work. He even said something about that in the Book of Genesis and it is taken for granted throughout the Old Testament. Even God's son Jesus was a carpenter in a little town and the first people who followed him were fishermen.

I don't know if there were potatoes to peel in those days. But everyone had his work to do, like watching the sheep in the fields or grinding up the grain to make bread. And everyone knew that whatever he did was important to someone.

I suppose it's easy to lose sight of this because not many of us get a chance to work in a garden or prepare and cook food. Most of us buy a package of frozen french fries and somehow or other we never think about those who planted the potatoes or those who peeled them. But every time you buy a package of frozen french fries you have helped a lot of people who work, and their work has given you nourishment so you can work. Even your mothers sometimes feel a little embarrassed when they produce a good cake and they will say, "Don't thank me, thank Sally Smith Cake Mix Company."

While I guess maybe not many of us will get a chance to work just for ourselves, we can remember that all the work can be of benefit to others. Like helping to do anything that makes the world a little better is good. God intended it that way no matter how small the job.

PRAYER: Dear God, sometimes when I feel so small, help me to see the importance of everything that I do. *Amen.*

How to Be a Saint

Do not think of yourselves more highly
than you should.
Rom. 12:3

There is a story of a nine year old boy who wanted to be a saint. He read the life stories of everyone he could find, but he liked St. Simon

Stylites the best. St. Simon lived for many years on top of a pole, sort of the first flagpole sitter. People made trips from many miles away just to see him. Some people thought he was some kind of nut or a weirdo. Others thought he was a holy man and came to get his blessing.

The boy figured he wanted to be another St. Simon. So he put a stool in the middle of the kitchen floor and said, "I'm going to stay here for forty years."

He soon found out that the path to becoming a saint was not easy, and had many roadblocks. Not the least of which was his mother, who said he was in the way and a first class nuisance. In fact, she made it so miserable for him that at the end of an hour he got off the stool and said, "It is very difficult to be a saint while living at home."

It's easy to put up a front when we are with people we don't know. It's hard to put into practice Christ's teachings with people who know us.

One of the best things you can say about Christ is his daily living matched his teaching, no matter where he was.

PRAYER: Help me to be true and on the level, wherever I am. *Amen.*

You Funny-Looking Jackass

> Let your eyes look directly forward and your
> gaze be straight before you.
> Prov. 4:25

There are lots of stories about the old Erie
Canal. One of them happened in Lockport. There
was a strong man, a blacksmith, who lived and
worked there. It was said he was the strongest
man in all of New York State. People used to
come from miles and miles to see the strong
man perform. It was said he could bend a thick
bar of iron, and that he could pick up and carry
a heavy horse.

Every Sunday afternoon great crowds came
to watch him do these things.

One day a funny-looking little man with a
funny-looking jackass came to the park and
said that he and his little jackass wanted to
challenge the strong man. Everybody began to
laugh and point and mock out the funny-looking
man and his jackass. The strong man thought
that it was the funniest thing he ever heard. He
just laughed and laughed.

But the little man said he wanted to try anyway. So the strong man took a good grip on the
harness that the little jackass was wearing and
said the test would begin.

The little jackass gave just a little pull and

everyone laughed some more. The strong man thought it was a great joke. The little man kept telling his little jackass to keep pulling. And he did—just a slow, steady pull, never letting up, just keeping a steady pull on the strong man.

That went on for a long time and people began to stop their laughing. The strong man's arms began to get sore and he stopped laughing. Still the funny-looking little jackass—with a gentle whisper from the funny-looking little man—kept up his steady pull. He just kept it up and kept it up, and the strong man's arms were getting sore. Pretty soon he couldn't take it anymore and he dropped the harness.

And the funny-looking little man and his funny-looking little jackass had beaten the strongest man in all New York State!

The jackass had learned from pulling barges on the canal for many years that it was not the sudden jerks that got those heavy barges moving, and kept them moving. What it took was a steady pull that never relaxed. That got them moving and kept them moving.

PRAYER: When we think it's time to give up, Lord, help us to keep a steady pull. *Amen.*

Busted Things

Behold, I make all things new.
Rev. 21:5

A lot of people who live on the seacoast of Maine make their living as lobster fishermen. The lobstermen put traps down into the deepest part of the water. They mark where their traps are by tying a long rope on the trap. On the other end they tie a block of wood, or sometimes a bottle.

The bottles come in many different colors, brown, green, red, or just plain clear glass. Sometimes the wind comes up and makes huge waves that may break the rope that holds the bottles to the traps. The bottles then float into shore and are broken to bits on the rocks. The waves keep right on pounding them, washing them back into the ocean and back again on to the shore.

This action makes the bottles into many odd and weird shapes and sizes. Eventually the action of the waves makes their edges round and smooth.

There was a man and his wife who used to go down to the shore and pick up the odd and weird shaped broken glass. Lots of people thought the man and his wife were odd and weird, too. They took the pieces of broken glass back to their cabin. There they made them into lamps, hot pads, and even into windows like you see in churches. When the light was turned on behind the windows they were beautiful, more beautiful than you can imagine.

Little did the lobster fishermen ever dream that the bottles they used to mark their traps would ever become beautiful lamps, windows, and hot pads.

And no one ever though that the broken glass that made the shore look like a dump and was so dangerous to walk on would ever serve a useful purpose. But when the broken glass was discovered by an artist, it became something of great beauty.

Most anybody could develop that idea into a sermon or "chapel talk".

Think how it is possible to take brokenness and turn it into a thing of great beauty.

So why don't you develop your own sermon? Be my guest.

PRAYER: Is turning busted things into useful things so hard, Lord? *Amen.*

The Project Manager

. . . as a good manager of God's different gifts.
1 Pet. 4:10

A steward in New Testament times was like the Project Manager who took care of the property. He was in charge of something that didn't really belong to him, but he was the boss just the same.

Did you ever think that God has put in our care certain abilities? For instance, some people have the ability to sing and make music. Some have the great ability to draw and produce art works. Some have a great ability in science and invention. Some have a great ability to care about other people, to share and understand, or as we sometimes say, provide a shoulder for somebody to cry on. No matter what your ability is, it really ought to be used in service to God and our fellowman. It doesn't make any difference, really, whether we have a lot of abilities or only a few. You, and you alone, have the responsibility to use them well.

In the Scripture lesson that we read it said that a good Steward has to be found faithful. A good automobile mechanic is one whose interest is in making an automobile, whether it is a hot-rod or a Cadillac, run well, and who takes pride in his work, and uses his ability.

Here are a few of the reasons people offer for not using the gifts God gives them:

The first is just plain old laziness.

The second is the fear that the job is too big for them, and that they will fail if they take it on.

The third is their feeling that the job they have a talent or a gift for is just not worth doing.

The fourth, and perhaps the most often used, is refusing to believe that each person's greatest responsibility is to do his very best with what he has.

PRAYER: Father, some of us don't have very many gifts to use, but help us to be clever enough to use what we have. *Amen.*

The Face

His face became as bright as the sun.
Matt. 17:2

Did you ever wonder what Christ really looked like? Seems like no two pictures we see are the same. There is good reason for that. Nobody does know what he looked like. All the pictures that you see are only what someone thinks he looked like. All the Bible says about him is, "His face did shine as the sun." That's all. Did you ever think about your face? Here is the way one person did:

"As a beauty I'm no shining star,/there are others more handsome by far./My face I don't mind it,/because I'm behind it,/It's the folks out in front that I jar."

Once when a young boy came down to breakfast, his father said, "You don't own your face." The young boy thought, "What's with him?" But his father really was right. The boy had a deep frown because he was down. But the way he looked made other family members feel way down, too.

Sometimes we say more by the look on our face than we do with words. Wonder what Christ looked like when he took those little kids on his knee? Or when he talked to the woman at the well? Or when he drove the crooks out of the temple? Or when he healed sick people? Or when he talked to Nicodemus or to Mary and Martha? Or when he said, "Father forgive them for they know not what they do"? Or what he looks like right now as he looks at us?

PRAYER: As we wonder, may we see our own looks. *Amen.*

From the Old Testament

Shook Up

. . . and he shall direct thy paths.
Prov. 3:6

You have all heard somebody say, "Don't fret over it." That's a word we don't use very often and when we do we are usually talking about something that is bugging us. Fret, bugged, scared, shook-up—they are all words that mean something is disturbing us inside. We are worried over something. That happens to all of us at times.

Some people get all shook-up when they get tired and discouraged. It is easy then to start fretting and worrying.

Sometimes we get shook-up when something hurts us. I don't mean the kind of hurt when we catch our finger in a door. I do mean the kind of hurt that comes when we try our very best to do something for someone else and everything goes wrong. Or maybe when someone that we love even more than we love ourselves goes wrong and we see how that person is hurting himself and us, too. It shakes us up. Then at times we get all shook-up because the things we dream about and plan for and sometimes work so hard for never really quite come our way.

We get shook-up because somehow we never

quite accept the fact that there are some things in life we can't change. Sometimes we get peeved at ourselves. You have heard someone say, "I can do anything that anybody else can." That is rather stupid, you know. For instance, I never could do very much as an artist. Yet I have known a lot of other people who could. In school my worst subject was math. I not only couldn't do it, I hated it. I was always one of the smallest persons in my class. In school I was the runt and in my platoon in the army. These things used to shake me up until one day a friend of mine helped me to see that that's the way things were and I just better accept it.

Getting all shook-up about things is really a waste of time. Often times it hurts us and keeps us from facing up to the facts that shake us up.

One of the best ways to keep from getting all shook-up about things is found in some words that were spoken by a psalmist a long time ago: "Trust in the Lord. Delight yourself also in the Lord. Commit your ways unto the Lord and he will direct your path."

PRAYER: In daily life, Jesus, may I take my problems one by one. *Amen.*

Danger!

God is our refuge.
Ps. 46:1

The other day a fellow said the world is a very dangerous place to live in. He is right, you know!

If you don't believe him, take a look at the headlines in the newspapers. People killed in an automobile accident or a train wreck or a plane crash, or in a war. Or maybe they get sick, or drunk, or a lot of other things. So why go on? What's the use. Let's play it safe.

Words like that are the words of a "cop-out," a doubter. God's man says, I may not know what is ahead of me, but somehow I am sure I can make it.

The astronauts stepped one morning into a rocket, waved goodby to a handful of friends and technicians who were standing near. Then with a roar they were off across space, hoping they would land on the moon. But they didn't know it. They really didn't know it. So for hours, even days, they flew through space with one aim and only one, and that was to land on the moon. You know the mission was accomplished without a crack-up. Did you also know they did it because they had help from a lot of other people, and a lot of faith in those other people, as well as themselves?

Sure, the world is a dangerous place, but there are a lot of things that nobody knows for sure. No pitcher in a baseball game ever knows, even five seconds before he throws the ball, what the batter will do with it. No golfer can tell you where his ball will land. That's true with your life, and mine. Tomorrow may be just another rotten day with all kinds of danger.

But we open the bag just the same. Why? Because within us there is faith, faith that looks into each new day and somehow wants to believe in God, and goodness. Perhaps it might even be that the world wouldn't be so dangerous if we developed that faith within us.

PRAYER: In a rotten mess of things, help us, God, to believe. *Amen.*

The Truth and Nothing But the Truth

Be sure your sin will find you out.
Num. 32:23

"Do you swear to tell the truth, the whole truth, and nothing but the truth?" If you have not already heard these words, you will when your trial comes up. It's called an oath. When the oath is administered you are asked to put your hand on a Bible. Why do you suppose that is? I guess to some people this seems kinda crazy like, and doesn't make much sense. Especially when a person doesn't plan to level anyway, Bible or no Bible.

Who thought up this idea? Where did it come from? The idea of an oath goes way back, man. It's supposed to be a way to make sure a witness is telling the truth—or else!

Over in Assam it used to be that a guy was asked to hold a spear and a tiger tooth in his hands. Then he would say, "If I'm not telling the truth may I die by one of these." In some parts of India it used to be that right behind where the witness stood or sat they kept a hungry tiger on a rope. If he told a lie, it was his last. And that's for sure.

As laws were developed there also had to be a way of being certain that people came clean. So they called upon a person to take an oath before God, and the Bible was used as a symbol. From this we get such expressions as, "So help me, God," or, "Honest to God," or, "May God strike me dead," or, "Cross my heart."

No one seems to be certain how people got started using the Bible in giving oaths. About all we know for sure is that the Hebrews used the Old Testament. And Christians continued it, I guess. But it's probably really because the Bible is the truth so people figured out that there was no greater thing to swear by to guarantee the truth. A test of its truth is the fact that people who fail to live by its teachings get goofy ideas about life and ways to live, and make a mess of things. Maybe that's one of the reasons there are lots of selfish people who just don't give a hoot about anyone else, or husbands or wives who just take off on each other and their kids.

It seems like the world is full of people who are always trying to give someone a "snow job", or "con artists" who think a lie is just a big joke. And somehow we make ourselves feel O.K. about it by saying, "I ain't the only one doing it". Sometimes I wonder who you can believe these days.

Listen, man! Anything that requires a lie just isn't that important. And that's no lie, chum! I guess, too that, no matter what I say, people are still going to go on lying—to others, to courts, to themselves, and even to God.

A long time ago, some people were thinking about getting away with things and how most of the time it sort of catches up with you in the end. You guessed that I'm talking about some people in the Bible. They came up with this idea, "Be sure your sins will find you out." Or they could have said, "My record caught up with me." Jesus said it this way, "Whatever a man sows, that shall he also reap." So what he says to us is that we sort of get caught up with sooner or later. And that's the truth, too.

So I guess the Bible is the truth, and there is good reason for using it to swear by.

PRAYER: For once in my life may I level with myself—and with others. *Amen.*

God Almighty!

How excellent is Thy name.
Ps. 8:1

Did you ever hear anybody say, "God Almighty," or at least something that sounds like it? Sometimes we say it when we hit our finger with a hammer, or when somebody tells us something that surprises us. But did you know that back of it there is some real meaning?

People say that God is almighty; that he is all-powerful; that there isn't anything that he can't do. People have been trying ever since the beginning of time to put into words how they feel about God and they have never quite been able to do it. Just like we can never really put into words how we feel when that hammer hits our finger!

When we say that God is almighty, that's pretty close, or it is at least as close as we can come to describing what God is like. But somehow our little minds can't quite understand what a God must be like who can create a world, who can start a life, and love and care about us.

Would it surprise you if I told you that there are some things that even God can't do? That he has limited his power? He limited himself when he decided to set up a world that is orderly and law-abiding. It operates by certain rules, such as, water always runs down-hill, and two plus two makes four, and that when apples fall off a tree they fall down and not up.

God puts some limits, too, when he gave people like you and me freedom of will to choose either good or evil. No doubt he could have done it another way. He could have made us into machines that are unable to think and can only do what he wants us to do. But instead he gave us the power to follow our own wills, whether we want to be good or, well, bad, or selfish and mean and nasty and stubborn. But remember, he also gave us the power to love, to

serve, to care and to be at peace with ourselves
and our fellowmen.

PRAYER: O God, since we have to choose because you have made us free, help us to
choose the right thing and to create the
kind of world we dream about. *Amen.*

Blowing His Top!

Train up a child in the way he should go,
and even when he is old he will not depart
from it.
Prov. 22:6

No one is a child here, of course. But that
doesn't mean we are too old to learn. For sooner
or later a man, if he is wise, discovers that life
has good days and bad days. Days when he is on
the bottom and days when he is on the top. He
learns that some days he has to give·a little and
other days take something. He learns that it
doesn't pay to blow his top but to let some
things go over his head like water off a newly
waxed car.

He learns that in losing his temper he usually
loses out. Carrying a chip on his shoulder usually only means there is wood higher up. Passing the buck turns out to be a boomerang. He

learns he is never such a big wheel that things can't go on without him. He learns that it doesn't do any harm to smile and say good morning even if it's a messy day.

He learns that snowing other people in the end means that he has given himself a con job. He learns that no man ever got to first base all by himself.

He learns not to worry when things go wrong because experience proves that if he always gives his best his average will break pretty well in his favor.

He learns that folks are not any harder to get along with in one place than another and getting along depends about 98% on ourselves.

PRAYER: Learning never stops. May we learn that to start with. *Amen.*

Stir Crazy

> This is the day the Lord has made;
> let us rejoice and be glad in it.
> Ps. 118:24

Here are some words that you have probably heard before.They are from the Book of Psalms.

I don't know if the psalmist had ever done any time in a joint or not, but if you think about his words you discover that he has learned how to do time because he has learned how to live one day at a time. This is a lesson well worth learning in everything that we do. It makes sense. No matter how hard you try you can't possibly live two days at a time. You have to take them as they come. Perhaps that old saying, "One thing at a time," had its beginning in the Book of Psalms.

It is wise to live just one day at a time because after all that's all that you have. A very wise man once said, "Yesterday has gone and tomorrow hasn't come yet." Someone else has put it this way, "Today is the tomorrow you worried about yesterday and all is well".

Perhaps we ought to live one day at a time because it is all we can handle.

In fact, if we would learn to handle one day at a time, we would be all right. The wino could stay sober one day at a time. The drug addict could probably manage to be clean for one day. The biggest liar around could probably level for one day, and the biggest crook could stay straight for one day. The most disappointed and heartbroken person in the world could probably endure his heartache for one day.

To be patient with yourself and with God for one day at a time will make it possible for all of us to say this is the day that the Lord has made. Let us rejoice and be glad in it.

PRAYER: We get up tight over so many things. Help us to stay cool, just for one day. *Amen.*

Watch It!

I almost quit, I nearly lost my footing.
Ps. 73.2

Have you ever been walking with someone when he stepped on a piece of ice or something that was slippery and started to fall and you would shout, "Watch it?" In a way that's what this verse from the Book of Psalms is all about. The man who wrote it is trying to show us how he came near falling and having a real tragedy.

I guess that's true of all of us. It's like when we look back over everything that's happened to us and have said, "Here's where I went wrong." The man in this psalm went wrong because he had such big ideas that when he began to compare them with the world around him, he became awfully discouraged. I suppose it's like what happens to us when we try to get a job and we can't, because of the color of our skin. Or when we see people being hurt because they are poor. Or when we see the world being ruined by pollution. Or somebody's life being ruined by booze or narcotics. Then what we are taught about this being God's world and full of beauty doesn't seem to check with the facts. That's when we slip and lose our footing.

But this man didn't lose his footing because by looking around he found an even stronger faith. And he did it in a way that sounds just too simple for us to believe. He said that he went to the sanctuary of God. In other words, he went seeking for God and he came to a new awareness of Him. He began to see that sometimes people who seem the most poor are inwardly the most rich, and the most rich are inwardly the most poor. He discovered that it is not God who has turned his back upon the world, but he and his fellow human beings. He discovered that if the world is to be a better place, he will have to help make it better.

Perhaps he is like the fellow who said he had seen the sign that read, "If you feel far away from God, who moved?"

PRAYER: If we feel far away from You, help us to discover who moved. *Amen.*

Half-Baked

Ephraim is a cake not turned.
Hos. 7:8

No doubt you have heard somebody being accused of being half-baked. That's not a new idea. It is recorded way back in the Old Testament days even though they didn't use the exact words.

What was wrong with this fellow Ephraim? Actually it was just that he could see only one side of any opinion. He was like a lot of people. They are not balanced. They have too much of one thing and not enough of another.

I don't suppose any of us want to be half-baked. We really want to be the full-rounded persons that God intended us to be. Here are some suggestions that may prevent you from becoming half-baked.

First of all, be caring about our brothers, for remember that Christ taught us that every man is our brother.

The second is to develop self-control so that when someone offers you that drink, or that fix, or whatever, you can say "No" and mean it and make it stick.

The third is to be serious in facing up to life's problems, but not so serious that the problems overwhelm you. The Bible tells us to learn both how to laugh and how to weep. But we sometimes forget that the laughing can be as important as the weeping.

The next is to be a dreamer, to plan for things you think you cannot do, to tackle jobs that you think are too big for you and yet, at the same time, to be a realist who learns his limits and lives within them.

And finally, be religious. To acknowledge God and Christ and your dependence upon them for life, for purpose, and for meaning in life is a big order. But so is life.

These things will help you become a well-rounded person and not somebody who is half-baked.

PRAYER: There are enough half-baked people in the world, Jesus. I want to be steady and whole. *Amen.*

Pick Yourself Up

> But David encouraged himself in the Lord his God.
> 1 Sam. 30:6

This part of the Bible tells the story of David. You always think of him as a great hero, and the man who wrote most of the Book of Psalms. But that is only part of the story.

Actually, he was a flop in a great many things. One time he lost all of his friends and then he lost everything he owned. He got up tight and just plain mad at the world and that's about how it was when these words were written. No one knows how David encouraged himself, so my guess is as good as anyone else's.

I don't suppose he spent a lot of time feeling sorry for himself and all that he had lost, and blaming everybody else for his troubles. Perhaps he began by taking stock of what he had left and then began to use that.

He didn't give up too quickly. Just because he failed once didn't mean that he was going to fail every time. He really believed in the possibilities of a brand new start. Who knows? He may have been the first member of the "second chance club."

But most important of all, Bible words themselves say that David encouraged himself in the Lord his God. To believe in God is the first step. To believe in ourselves is the second. To believe in oneself and in God and put them together is the third and always successful step. It can keep one from cracking up and going to pieces and blowing his mind.

That is why David wrote, "Trust in the Lord with all your heart and lean not to your own understandings. In all your ways acknowledge him and He will direct your path."

PRAYER: When we are down in the dumps or on a bad trip, help us to pick ourselves up. In Jesus' name. *Amen.*

Mind Your Own Business

As thy servant was busy here and there, he was gone.
1 Kings 20:40

This verse is a part of an Old Testament parable. A parable is a story told to illustrate a certain truth about life.

The story is about a man who had been captured in war and became a P.O.W. He was very important, and the soldier who was to guard him was told this. He was warned that if the prisoner escaped he would have to pay with his own life.

But when it came time for the guard to turn the P.O.W. over to the commanding officer, they discovered that the P.O.W. had escaped. When the guard was asked what happened he realized that he had been busy doing a lot of jobs and had forgotten to pay attention to the P.O.W. So he said, "As thy servant was busy here and there, he was gone."

That's like a lot of the messes we get into. We don't plan it that way. They sort of just happen while we are busy with all sorts of things, most of which just really don't matter that much. The guard was just like a lot of us. He had been so busy that he didn't have time to mind his own real business, guarding the P.O.W.

Perhaps this story tells us that one of the really big things we can do in life is to mind our own business. We all have been given some kind of a special talent and God expects us to use it. Using it wisely is minding your own business.

Minding our own business brings several benefits, too. One of them is spiritual and mental health. I suppose a lot of people are sick, a lot of people lose faith, and are up tight over lots of things. And a lot go on booze or pot because they have no hope, or maybe because they have no purpose or values in life. Finding them, finding ourselves, is our business.

Then too, when we're busy minding our own business we will not be butting into the business of others. Nobody loves a meddler, someone who is always sticking his nose into somebody else's business. That, by the way, is always sure to get us into a mess, and keep us busy in the wrong way.

As thy servant was busy here and there, he was gone. The guard was busy about the wrong things.

PRAYER: Keep us, Lord, from minding everybody's business but our own. *Amen.*

Stories of Quiet Wisdom

Who Are You?

We all make many mistakes.
James 3:2

When you were a little kid did you ever play that game called, "Let's Pretend"? And get all dressed up in your mother's or father's clothes? That's fun when you are a kid. Unfortunately there are a lot of people who go right on playing it all through life and never really accept who they are. Sometimes they spend so much time worrying that somebody is better than they are, at least they think they are, that they never come to grips with themselves. They get as stupid as the donkey I heard about in a story a long time ago.

It goes something like this;

There was a donkey who while eating grass in a field, struck oil and suddenly got very rich. Now this donkey immediately began to get big ideas so he quit associating with donkeys and began to run with the horses. He went to a plastic surgeon and had his ears trimmed and pulled down so they looked like the ears of a horse. He got along quite well until one night, after he had had too many drinks, he decided that he would sing a solo for the crowd that he was with. Now, donkeys make the worst noise in all the animal kingdom and so everybody knew immediately what he really was.

At first he was a bit upset over the fact that he had been found out. But later on when he got back with his own fellows, he said he had discovered a new happiness.

Accepting ourselves for whom we are and what we are and developing a sense of pride that we are children of God, may be the greatest accomplishment of our life.

PRAYER: Jesus, may I make one life just a little better—my own. Then help someone else. *Amen.*

The Bears

Walk in the way of insight.
Prov. 9:6

Two bears lived in Yellowstone Park in Wyoming in the western part of our country. Both were born about the same time, and they played together as little cubs. They tried many different ways to show which one was stronger than the other and to prove who had the biggest muscle.

One great summer day one of the cubs was walking through the woods when he stopped by a small tree and stretched to his highest height. He shouted, "I'm the biggest bear in these woods." He made a scratch in the bark of the tree to prove it.

About a month later his friend came by and saw the scratch. So he stood on his hind legs and stretched to his highest height and made a scratch and said he, and not his friend, was the biggest bear in the park.

Before long, the first bear came by again. He saw the scratch his friend had made so he made another just a little higher up, and said, "I'm still the biggest bear in the park." Then the second bear came by again. He saw the scratch and made another one, and said he was the biggest bear in the park. This thing went on all summer until there was so many scratches in the tree that the tree died. And nothing was proved.

PRAYER: Help me, God, to understand the feelings of others. *Amen.*

The Fire

The hand of the diligent makes rich.
Prov. 10:4

All people have legends as ways of telling stories that are important. Sometimes they are used to pass on history and other times to pass on some great idea that will be helpful to a person.

There is an Indian legend about the way to make fire was discovered. It tells about two Indian children who were playing near their home. Their mother was starting to fix their dinner, when she discovered the fire had gone out and she had no way to cook the meat. Most of the time the fire was kept burning for days at a time. But somehow it had been allowed to go out.

Nomo's mother—one of the boys was named Nomo—called to him and told him to go down to Red Feather's wigwam and bring back a burning stick from Red Feather's fire. But Nomo and his brother were having a good time playing with their father's tools. Their father had many interesting toools because he made jewelry. One of these tools was a hard stone drill that was used to make holes in beads. Nomo was using it to drill a hole in a block of wood. The drill went around and around with great speed as Nomo pushed and pulled the bow that held the drill. And Nomo pushed and pulled harder than ever now, so he could get the hole done before his mother blew her stack and made him go to get the fire.

Pretty soon the wood began to smoke and before long the little pile of sawdust from the hole caught on fire. Nomo shouted to his mother to look at what he had done. His mother was pretty shook up about seeing what he had done. But she lighted the fire with it.

Nomo had made a great discovery when he was not looking for it. Before this time people had to borrow fire from their neighbors. But after Nomo's discovery they began to light their own fires whenever they needed to.

No one knows if that legend is true. But Indian parents told it to teach their children to be alert and caring and to use what they had for everybody's good.

PRAYER: It is easy to forget that there are people who are poor and hungry, cold and sick. Help me, Jesus, to be able to use my abilities to help other people. *Amen.*

Man, Is He Hard to Get Along With!

> . . . if you love only people who love you.
> Matt. 5:46

Did you ever meet a person that no matter what you did—it was wrong? And all of the time you were trying to be helpful. Until at last you say, "Man, is he ever hard to get along with!"

There is a very old story about that problem. One day the wind was blowing about and saw a boy trying to fly a kite. The boy would run a little and the kite would go up in the air; he would stop moving, and the kite would fall down. The wind thought, "I'll just help that boy." So the wind went over and blew as hard as he could. The kite went up into the air and the boy laughed and called, "Thank you, good wind, for making my kite fly." This made the wind glad. He got a big bang out of seeing little kids happy.

The wind found another boy who was walking along a road. He looked like he had "had it" or something. So the wind said, "I think I'll try to cheer him up." The boy didn't have a kite. So the wind blew his cap off and flew across the road with it. The boy got mad about that and started chasing his cap, and shouting, "I hate this stupid wind."

The wind was so surprised that he dropped

the cap. The boy picked it up, put it on, and went home real mad.

The wind thought, "That's a funny thing. One boy likes to play with me. The other hates me. I guess some people are just hard to get along with."

Sure, it's a silly story. But most of the time the things that make it hard to get along with a person are silly, too.

Here are some ideas that Christ gave us that may help us get along with people:

"You have heard that it was said, 'Love your friends, hate your enemies.' But now I tell you, 'Love your enemies, pray for those who mistreat you. . . .'

'Why should you expect God to reward you if you love only people who love you? . . . and if you speak only to your friends, have you done anything out of the ordinary?'"

PRAYER: It's easy to be hard to get along with, Lord. That's not for me. *Amen.*

Get Off My Back

Show a gentle attitude toward all.
Phil. 4:5

Did you ever say, or hear anyone say, "Get off my back?" There is a story—it's an oldie—that may tell us where that phrase, "Get off my back," got started. It goes like this.

There was a horse who had a pasture all to himself. One day a big buck deer came into the pasture. He said he had a right to eat there and he was going to claim it. More than that, he was taking all the best places. The horse got pretty "up tight" about this and tried to find a way to get the deer out. He went to a man and asked his help in getting rid of the deer. The man agreed but he made a demand. He must be allowed to put a bridle on the horse and ride on his back. They agreed, shook hands, and the deal was made.

Together they drove the deer out of the pasture. But when it was over, the man refused to take off the bridle and to get off the horse's back. The horse discovered that the man had become his master and he could not get rid of him. The man was "bugging" the horse.

That bit about bugging is what we mean when we say, "Get off my back." Lots of things "bug" people, like booze, narcotics, laziness, selfishness, and lots of other things.

We all have something or someone "on our back" sometimes. The important thing is that we don't lose control and take a bit in our mouth like the horse. There are some words—like the story—that are oldies. But they are still helpful. Here they are:

". . . fill your minds with those things that are good and deserve praise. Things that are true, noble, right, pure, lovely, and honorable. Put into practice what you have learned and received . . . and the God who give us peace will be with you."

PRAYER: When we feel empty, Jesus, fill us with good things. *Amen.*

A Big Blast

Stop judging by outward standards.
John 7:24

Did you ever get into a big blast and then discover that it was over a pretty small thing, something that didn't really matter?

Did you ever go to the movies and see a story about some knights?

Once two of them were coming down a path

from opposite directions, and they saw a shield tied to the branch of a tree. They didn't know who owned it or why it was left hanging there, so the first knight said "Who owns this white shield?" And the second knight said "What do you mean, white? It's black." That teed off the first knight and he began to shout, "What do you think I am? Blind, or a fool, or something?" And so they got into a real blast about it. They even began to draw their weapons.

Then a third knight happened to come along. After hearing what the blast was all about he took a look at the shield, first from one side and then from the other, and then he suggested, "Instead of fighting, why don't you change places?" When they did that they discovered that one side of the shield was black and the other was white. That made them both feel rather stupid. So they shook hands and went on their way as good friends as ever.

Half the misunderstandings and fights that break up families and neighborhoods and friends come from doing what this Bible text tells us not to do—judge not from outward appearance.

Judging from outward appearance is not a true way of judging. It certainly is not a just way, nor is it a safe way.

PRAYER: O Lord, help us to see things from the other fellow's shoes. *Amen.*

Don't Lose Them

O give thanks unto the Lord.
Ps. 118:1

Here's another one of those folk tale things that gives you something to think about.

Once there was a rich and kind man who had a servant whom he liked very much.

When the rich man was taken sick and very near death, he called his servant and said he wanted to give him a gift.

"After I die," he said, "you will want to take a trip around the world and you will need a lot of things. Here is a magic bag and in it is everything you will need. I want to give you something else. I give you four magic words which I have written on this piece of paper. I want you to keep them in the bag but I also want to whisper them in your ear. Don't lose them or forget them. As long as you remember them your bag will stay full."

Soon after, the old man died. Sure enough, the servant set out on his journey and he travelled over all the world to places where it was hot, and where it was cold. And he always found in his bag the things he needed. He kept the four magic words in his mind and written on the piece of paper he kept in the bag.

As he traveled over the world he began to think less about the magic words. In fact, some days he didn't think about them at all and it was not long before he forgot them.

One day as he was going down a very steep hill, he slipped and fell. When he picked up his bag there were only a few things left in it. "Never mind," he said, "I will say the magic words and it will be full again." But when he tried to say them, he discovered he had forgotten them. Even the slip of paper they were written on had been lost when he fell. Now he was in a real mess. His bag was almost empty and the words were forgotten.

As he traveled he came into a small town and asked the Mayor what the magic words were. The Mayor said they are, "I wish I had, I wish I had." So the servant went on his way and before long he began repeating those words, "I wish I had." But they got him nothing.

Before long he met another man and he asked him if he knew what the magic words might be, and the man replied, "I sure do. All you have to say is, 'Give me some more, give me some more.'" And so he repeated them, but nothing happened.

The servant kept on his trip. Before long he met some kids who were crying because they were cold and hungry. The servant felt sorry for them and he began to wish that his bag were full. He discovered that there was a sandwich and some fruit left, so he gave them to the children. It made him feel good inside to know that he had been able to help even a little bit and he found himself saying, "I thank you, Lord. I thank you, Lord." As he spoke those words he remembered that they were the four words the old man had given him. And when he picked up his bag, he saw that it was full to the brim.

Maybe the meaning behind the story is not as weird as you think.

PRAYER: May we always remember that we have something to share with other people, and be thankful, O God, with our hearts and voices. *Amen.*

The Double Con Job

Lying lips are an abomination to the Lord:
but they that deal truly are his delight.
Prov. 12:22

Here is another one of those folk tales that really sounds pretty silly. In fact, it sounds outright stupid. But before you turn it off, at least check it out, for beyond the stupidity there just might be something being said.

One morning a fox heard a rooster crowing. So the fox ran up and said, "You crow very well, Mr. Rooster," and the rooster was greatly pleased and crowed over and over again.

The fox said, "You really do crow well, but I'll bet you can't crow standing on one leg." The rooster said, "I certainly can," and he did. "That's great," said the fox, "but you can't stand on one leg and shut one eye and crow." But the rooster could, and he did.

Then the fox said, "I'll bet you can't stand on one leg and shut two eyes and crow." So the rooster shut both eyes, stood on one leg and started to crow. And before you could snap your fingers the fox jumped, caught the rooster and ran away with him.

The fox stopped under a great big tree, put the rooster on the ground and held him with his paws and said to the rooster, "I fooled you that time. You are going to be a dinner for a true gentleman."

"Are you a gentleman?" asked the rooster. "I am that," said the fox. "Then," said the rooster, "you will wash your hands before you eat. All true gentlemen wash their hands before eating." "So do I," said the fox. "I'm going to wash them now." With that he let go of the rooster and the rooster promptly flew up into the tree. And there the rooster crowed, "First you fooled me, then I fooled you."

I suppose there are lots of things you could say about a stupid story like that. Like it's hip to keep out of dangerous company, or maybe when you begin to play tricks on someone you are liable to meet someone who goes you one better, and you get left. The story is sort of like a double con job.

PRAYER: We ask your help, Jesus, to think before we act. *Amen.*

From the New Testament

The Rat Race

He wasted his money in reckless living.
Luke 15:13

At almost every rap session a person is in, sooner or later the conversation gets around to "bread" and soon we are talking about people who have "made it" and people who "haven't made it". Before long a few people become aware that no one is ever satisfied. The people we accuse of "having it made" are trying to get something better and the people who haven't yet "made it" are trying awfully hard to "make it".

That sounds real mixed up, but it really describes the rat-race we are all caught in. And any rat-race is a mighty confusing thing.

Actually the rat-race isn't anything new. Jesus talked about the young fellow who came from a home where they had plenty of "bread". His parents were wealthy, so the young fellow had almost anything he wanted in hats and clothes, or food, or the latest model camel, or whatever it was they travelled with in those days. It seemed like he had everything that he wanted. But inwardly he knew, better than anybody else, that something was missing. He was "up tight", but he really wasn't sure what caused it.

It is a strange thing but sometimes the people

that have the most are the most aware that deep inside there is still something missing. So they start running without being quite sure what they are running after. So they run for dope, or for sex, or for booze, or popularity, or for some kind of a thrill. I suppose you could say they want to do their "thing", but they don't really know what their "thing" is.

It doesn't really tell us in this Bible story where this young fellow went. But if you let your mind run a little you could probably think of him being in a "go-go joint", or a "strip joint". You could probably think of him "blowing his mind" or getting "stoned". No doubt he thought he was "living it up".

You have heard it said that everything has its ending and that's the way it was with him. One day he discovered his pockets were empty. He had "blown his roll".

This fellow made an effort to think and for the first time to think straight. And he came to the conclusion that there was only one thing to do. That was to go home and level with his father who was waiting for him and ready to forgive him.

That forgiving bit is one of the things people who are always on the run are looking for, and that's exactly what Christ does when we come to him. As long as we are willing to give up what we are doing that we know is wrong, he forgives our past and his strength and power come into our lives and help us to begin again.

PRAYER: May we remember, Jesus, that you are waiting for us. *Amen.*

Right On!

> Seek, and you will find.
> Luke 11:9

A lot of people tell me that they pray and nothing happens. I have felt that way myself at times, as a matter of fact.

Some people cop-out on prayer by saying, "What can you get by praying that you can't get yourself?" So they don't need to pray.

Perhaps that comes out of that "kid stuff" thinking that God is like some visiting uncle or grandfather who likes to take you down to the neighborhood store to buy you a piece of candy. Somehow we get the idea that God is just a "give-me" man.

Perhaps the first step in getting this kid stuff idea straightened out is to look to the Bible and see what it says about prayer. Do you remember the part of the Scripture that we read? If you ask a father for a fish, would he give you a snake? Or if you asked him for egg, would he give you a bug? Well, any kid knows the right answer to that question. Then it goes on and speaks of how much more God will give the Holy Spirit to those who ask him.

The Holy Spirit. That sounds like a switch, one of those things when you change the subject. Let's look at it this way. It is safe to say that God is concerned and cares about you and the things that interest you, and the things that help make you happy and contented. One of the things that God's Holy Spirit does is help you to understand yourself and the world you live in. That's why we preachers are always talking about the Holy Spirit taking over your life.

When somebody is griping to me that he didn't get very good grades in school, and says, "Where was God then?", maybe the answer is that God was there all the time and you didn't do your part by studying. Or, when you lose your job, maybe you didn't do your part by doing a full day's work. What I'm saying, I guess, is that if you don't do your part then maybe it is time to stop blaming God for what you are unwilling to do.

Prayer is a lot more than just holding out your hand and saying to God, "Give me". It is more than some words you repeat before you go to bed at night or before you get into a dentist's chair. And especially before you go over to Court for sentence! Prayer is the whole way in which you live, the way you conduct your life, the attitude which you have toward other people.

If you think prayer is just asking God for something and then sitting around and waiting for it to drop from the sky, all I can say to you, man, is, "Get comfortable, it's a long wait". If you believe that prayer is asking God for guidance, for help, for direction, and then you go about doing your part to bring about an answer, then all I can say to you is, "Right on, man, right on."

PRAYER: Father, may we do our part. *Amen.*

Thanks for Nothing!

Be helpful to one another.
Col. 3:13

Did you ever wake up in the morning and have the feeling that it's going to be a great day? Of course there are other times when you feel like the world is going to cave in on you, and you fret and fuss. But most of the time you know it is great to be alive.

We have friends who really care and most of us have parents who really care.

We know that we are wonderfully made. We have minds that learn and grow. We have a pair of hands that a million bucks can't make and we have eyes that can see and a heart that can love.

And we live in America, a nation that is great and good. It has its faults and failures, but most of us wouldn't swap this country with any spot on earth.

Then there is the other side, too!

Did you ever have a toothache or break a bone? It hurt, didn't it? Did you ever feel like everybody in the world turned his back on you, including God? It hurt, didn't it? Why is there so much suffering in the world? Doubt if any of us will ever be big enough to understand and know the answers to that one any more than a fish can know everything there is to know about water. But God has put something in us that helps us stand on our feet and meet suffering when it comes.

Did you ever think that maybe there is something we can be thankful about even in suffering? The ability to feel is a pretty important thing. When we know what it is to hurt ourselves, we can sense other people's hurts. From this feeling and sensing of how the other fellow feels have come a lot of kindly steps which have taken us beyond cruelty. Perhaps we ought to pray that God will make us even more sensitive of other people's hurts. Seems like everybody is getting to be a number these days—a number on a report card in school, on a social security card, a number in a jail, a number on a driver's license and even a number if you are a patient in a hospital; numbers until we feel totally lost and that's the worst kind of suffering of all. But suffering can be the greatest teacher that we can have.

When suffering comes, let us not feel sorry for ourselves but find a way to put our hand into the hand of God that we may use our own suffering to answer the needs of others, and to share with them.

PRAYER: We really want the world to be better. Help us to make suffering easier for someone else. *Amen.*

You Must Choose

If God is for us, who can be against us?
Rom. 8:31

Anybody can feel sorry for himself and think that he doesn't really amount to very much. It doesn't make much difference whether a person is wino filled with the cheapest "slippery pete" or a rich man whose pockets bulge with money.

There are a lot of problems that everyone meets and everyone meets a lot of difficulties. Sometimes we do not have an opportunity to solve the difficulty, or problem. Or perhaps we may not even be clever enough to do it.

You already know how it is with a wino or a narcotic addict trying to escape from his problems. He soon discovers that the problems he tries to escape from or ignore only grow worse.

When problems come, and they will, you have no choice but to choose. Some people try to solve their problems by choosing narcotics, or liquor. Some try running away and some try to kid themselves that the problem does not exist. All they really do is add another problem. The most important choice of all is that you must choose to discover who you really are; to discover that you are a son of God; that you are created in God's image; that there is within you the possibility of changing yourself. To choose to add faith in God, in Christ, and in yourself is what these words from the Scripture are all about.

PRAYER: When we know what it is all about, help us to choose and have the guts to stick by it. *Amen.*

The Age of Aquarius

You have told me the truth.
John 4:18

Have you heard some one singing, "It is the dawning of the age of Aquarius"? What they are talking about is the dawning of a new day. In troubles like our own, who doesn't think about a new day? Have you got around to do much thinking about all the revolutions that are going on? Some people call them social, others call them political. Some call them spiritual. People are beginning to be aware that there is such a thing as human brotherhood and our responsibility for our neighbors, the forgiveness of sins, the use of raw materials and the good life.

All of these things get talked about in "the revolution." Maybe they don't say forgiveness of sins, but they do talk about "hang ups" by which they really mean sin, in most cases. Sometimes I guess that's really what a church is all about.

Or should be about. It's what Christianity is all about. It's had its share of revolutions through the Gospel. It started schools and hospitals; it established social agencies to help people who are oppressed; it has sent people to help the poor all over the world and even provided chaplains in jails. There are more church related youth programs in the inner city than are run by any other kind of group. Churches and preachers have always been leaders in every social change in the history of our country.

Even in these days when it seems like everybody is out to get the church, it's ready to lay down its life if need be, for the world that God loves. Churches and church people have always been trying to help people, sometimes worrying about them, and sometimes sticking their necks out and getting clobbered by other people.

You can find fault with the church and with Christian people if you want. That's all right with me. But just be sure that you talk about the other side. When you put us on trial, just treat us with the fairness that you want to be treated with in your trial. Anyone can tear down. It takes guts to see the total picture.

PRAYER: Help us to see things like they really are before we make judgment. *Amen.*

Use It, Man!

You have been faithful.
Matt. 25:21

You've heard preachers talking about talents, haven't you? Maybe at a school, or a camp, or maybe at a club you have heard of talent shows. What's a talent? A talent is something that you can do, perhaps better than anyone else. At least it is something that you can do better than anything else you can do. Or maybe we can just say it is one of your strong points. Another word for talent would be an ability.

Since I am a minister and this is a chapel you are probably ready for what I am going to say now. Your talent, or ability, or strong points come from God.

That's not a very new idea. People have been talking like that for thousands of years so I can't blame you if you are saying "So what's new, man?" The new part is really thinking about the story that is told in the Scripture we have read. The important part of this story is not that two fellows doubled the money they had been given. The important thing is that one man didn't even bother to try. He just copped out.

I wonder what would happen if that cop-out had tried and failed and returned less than the money he had been given? Somehow I've got the feeling that the boss would have rewarded him just the same, because there is only one thing worse than failing and that's not to try.

I suppose all of us have limited abilities. Maybe we are just the one talent guys. But the best way to keep something is to use it.

Maybe a talent is like an automobile tire. It rots faster when we leave it in the cellar than it does when we run it on an automobile.

PRAYER: May we learn to use well what we have. *Amen.*

Where Is God At?

God is love.
1 John 4:8

Did you ever wonder where God is at? Wouldn't it be simple if he were to just stand here in front of us just once? Why does he keep himself hidden from us, forcing us to try to find our way in understanding what he is like?

But wait a minute. Have you ever seen somebody you loved? Sure, you say. But haven't you only seen their body in which they live and through which they show themselves? When you think about it, you see a hand, or a face;

but like you've heard it said, they are only flesh, bones and muscle. They are not really the one you love. Isn't it a fact that you have never seen them actually and never will? For instance, have you ever seen their love for you; their regard for you; their thoughts for you; their purpose for you?

Maybe if you think about it that way it will help you understand what and where God is. In the world about us somebody caring for you; somebody doing something for you even though they didn't have to do it; or when you go out of your way to give a friend a hand, that is where God lives and how he shows himself.

When you think about it that way you don't always have to think that God is up in Heaven. Like the churches have been saying all the time, God is here now. He is all around us and in us. He is even closer than breathing. He is in the acts of kindness, of thoughfulness, of regard, of love. Maybe that is why the Bible itself says that God is love.

PRAYER: May we find you, O God, in the kind of lives that we live and in Christ our Lord. *Amen.*

Satellites

We have left our homes to follow you.
Luke 18:28

Do you know what a satellite is? If you look in a dictionary you will probably find something like this: "A satellite is an attendant body revolving about a larger one." How is that for a mouthful? Maybe you can think of it like this. Downtown there is a big bank building. In the neighborhood where you live there is a branch bank, so the branch bank is a satellite of the downtown bank that we call the main office. Or we could say that the branch bank is the attendant body revolving around a larger one. The branch bank isn't the boss. It can't do anything that it wants to do. It takes its direction from the downtown bank.

The people whom Jesus called disciples might be called the first satellites of Jesus. They found real meaning for their lives only when they revolved around Jesus. They were just ordinary people like we are who found themselves attracted to a leader and they decided to follow him. They gave up all that they were doing and found themselves almost as if they had been made all over again. And they came to be called people who turned the world upside down. As long as they stayed in tune with Jesus they accomplished many great things.

There were some who heard about Jesus but did not follow him. They didn't find their orbit so they soared off into their own space and were never heard of again. Those who followed the example of Jesus found real meaning in their lives as satellites taking their direction and inspiration from Jesus whom they called "Lord" and "Master."

PRAYER: We ask, Jesus, that we may place you at the center of our lives. May all our thoughts and our actions keep us close to you. *Amen.*

The Plan*

> Everything must be done in a proper and orderly way.
> I Cor. 14:40

Within you is an ability for much greater accomplishment than you may think you are able to manage. There is hidden power in your life that can drive you through problems and carry you over those times that are bound to come when the easiest thing is to cop out.

---

*Prepared by Roger Hawthorne

Here is a six point plan that may help you tap your hidden power.

1. Planning. Plan your activities, everything you do, before you do them.

2. Attitude. Expect to be successful and work toward that end. Look and act as though success is completely assured. Work as though failure is impossible.

3. Budget. Budget your time. Know its value.

4. Positive values. Always think in terms of how things can be improved, of how better methods can be developed.

5. Flexibility. Keep calm. Be adaptable to innovation and change. People who are flexible live longer.

6. Think. Thinking is the most important job you will ever have. Develop and use this skill daily.

PRAYER: May we, too, do things in order. *Amen.*

What Are You?

For God loved the world so much. . . .
John: 3:16

Did anyone ever tell you that you have a twin? Or maybe you have run into somebody that you mistook for some person that you knew? There is an old saying that everyone has a double.

That's not really quite true because in the whole world there is no one who is exactly like you are. Sometimes it is possible to look like someone else. But deep inside you are unique. The word "unique" simply means, "one of a kind."

Sometimes we wish we could be someone else, or maybe like somebody else. Sometimes we wish we lived some place else in the world. Once in a while I hear somebody say he wishes he had never been born.

Pop-eye the Sailor in the comic strip used to say, "I am what I am and that's all that I am." And he was right. Maybe that is because God made us what we are and so we have to learn to come to grips with it.

That is one of the reasons some people say that school teachers, preachers, and parents as well as friends, are sometimes God's servants. They help us to understand ourselves and to know where we are strong and where we are weak. Although it is God's love that helps us to change our weaknesses.

There is an old story about a girl who had a pet pig. She used to scrub the pig, use all kinds of sweet-smelling soap, and put a big red ribbon around its neck. But as soon as she let the pig go it headed back for the mud and rolled in it.

The girl was only changing the outward appearance. Really to change a person and to make him what God wants him to be, you have to change the inside. That's what Christianity is all about. That's what Christ is all about: changing people on the inside. That is why Jesus told so many stories about things that people could understand.

While it is true that you are unique and different from anyone else in the world, you can become what God wants you to become.

He wants us to become filled with his love and peace. We are what we are, it is true. But what are we? We are children of God.

PRAYER: May we know ourselves, Lord, and what we are. *Amen*.

Cut It!

You must live the rest of your earthly lives controlled by God's will.
I Pet. 4:2

Cut it! Here are some words that we have all heard a lot. They have different meanings, of course, to different people.

Sometimes we use these words when we are angry, or upset or disgusted. I suppose they are words we could use when we think about the kind of world that we live in, where there seems to be so much injustice and racism and poverty, and people being treated like so much garbage.

It is not always easy to say in a situation like that that there is a God and that God is love. We are all tempted to ask, "You want me to believe there is a God in the middle of this mess?"

So, okay, how about looking at it this way? They are building a new bridge for the new expressway downtown. What if everybody working on that bridge decided to do it his own way and forget the plan that has been made? It would be a mess, that's what it would be. In a way that is what's been happening. People have just been going their own way and never bothering with anyone else. Worse than that. Some of them have not even seemed to know that there is a plan for living.

Like we always say in a chapel service that God's plan for us in living is found in the Bible. We know that it works well, because Christ, whom some of us call our Lord, lived according to that plan.

Unfortunately, a lot of people prefer to live by their own plan. When things don't work out as they think they should, they get mad and disgusted and decide that nothing will work, not even God's plan. So they say, "Cut it." And they, and sometimes whole communities, get boxed in and there is no way out except by people fighting for their own plans and stepping all over other people as they try to win.

But what about you? Do you say, "Cut it!" And then try to shift the blame for your own failures onto someone else?

PRAYER: It's easy to rap with friends about our problems, Lord. It's so hard to follow plans. *Amen.*

Who's Got a Halo?

Come with me.
Matt. 4:19

Did you ever go by a church and see a sign, St. Peter's Church, St. Paul's, or St. Mary Magdalene's, or whatever? Usually we think of the people the churches were named for as being not really human, and we forget that there was a time when they walked on the earth just like we do.

Did you ever really think about the people whom Christ called to be his disciples?

There was John. Now there was a real mean

one. He had a terrible temper. It was so bad that everybody called him the Son of Thunder. He was the kind of person who would give you a piece of his mind before he even knew if he could spare it.

And there was a fellow named Thomas. He didn't believe anything that anybody told him, no matter who it was. He had a lot of trouble trusting people. When he saw Christ after the Resurrection, he wouldn't believe it was him until he put his hand in his side and the print of the nails in his hand. That's where we got the idea of "a doubting Thomas."

Peter was the type of fellow who would smash you one right in the face. In fact, he did cut off a guy's ear. If anybody ever had a low boiling point, he was it. And what about Paul? He had one ambition in life and that was to kill off every Christian he could find. And Mary Magdalene, they considered her to be lower than an alley cat.

Then something happened to all of them. They came face-to-face with Jesus Christ. And John, instead of being the Son of Thunder, became the disciple whom Jesus loved. And Thomas became a strong, courageous and faithful man. And Peter lost his jumpiness and became a respected and trusted leader. And Paul got a new ambition. Instead of stamping out Christians, he became the greatest missionary for the faith. Mary Magdalene changed from a woman of the streets to one of the most beautiful persons in all of literature. And all I can say to you today is that the power of Christ to change lives is still available.

PRAYER: O Christ, help me to find you and know you and be what you want me to be. *Amen.*

Practicing and Preaching

I have not come to do away with them,
but to give them real meaning.
Matt. 5:17

Bible teachings don't mean a thing if we don't practice them!

Once a person has decided he wants to live God's way, he can't be boxed in. That's because we live in a world of other people—some good, some bad, some who just don't care.

Sometimes religious people have shut themselves away in caves and hermit huts in the woods and sometimes in big apartment houses. But Jesus stayed where the people were. Some people got mad at him and called him "a friend of sinners". He spent his time helping other people.

He saw some of the things that were beating people down, like greed and sickness, racism and violence, poverty and poor education, and lots of other things. He knew how much these things hurt people. Jesus taught in their place love and good will, brotherhood and peace, and that everybody was important to God. He taught how important it was to love even people that other people push around. Here are his own words: "I tell you, then, that you will be able to enter the Kingdom of heaven only if you are more faithful than the teachers of the Law and the Pharisees in doing what God requires." When we follow Christ we must do more than the average person. When a person has done more than his share because he is concerned about a person, then he really does care. Then we are putting Bible teachings into practice.

PRAYER: Help me, Lord, to say and do and practice my faith. *Amen.*

Have a Good Time, Man!

Rejoice always.
1 Thess. 5:16

Did you ever say, "Have a good time", or, "Have a good weekend", or, "Have a good day"? Or something like that?

They used to say the same thing in the Bible times, only they used different words like, "Rejoice always." That covers the day and the week, the month and maybe even the year. But what they were really talking about was all of life.

Maybe this Bible verse is interesting because just about everybody I ever have known wants to have fun. Nobody wants to be that poor guy you see in a cartoon in a magazine crawling in the middle of a desert looking for water. Unless I'm all mixed up, God really does want everyone to be happy, to be joyful, content, and to have a good time.

That's because cheerfulness and joyfulness are good for both physical and spiritual health. Nobody enjoys good spiritual health if he is always gloomy and down in the dumps. The next time you are looking at a Bible, try finding out how many times the word "rejoice" appears. Here are some quotes from the Bible: "Be glad in the Lord and rejoice. Shout for joy all you that are upright in heart." Another one: "Rejoice in the Lord always. And again I say, Rejoice." Listen to this: "These things have I spoken unto you that my joy might remain in you and that your joy might be full."

God wants us to have a good time in life because he knows to be gloomy is neither good for us nor our fellow men, but most of all because he loves us.

PRAYER: May we learn that you created laughter, too. *Amen.*

Grow Up, Man!

I put away childish things.
1 Cor. 13:11

How many times has somebody said to you, "Why don't you grow up, man?" Or maybe you said it to somebody else.

All of us, I suppose, are growing up all of our lives. It's called maturity.

These words were written by a man named Paul, so let's take a look and see what signs he gave that he had become a man. One of the things a baby does is cry a lot. But becoming a man doesn't mean that we put away our tears, it just means that we don't cry over little things any longer. It means that instead of our lives being self-centered and thinking only of ourselves, we begin to think of other people and care about them, and weep with them, and laugh with them, and stand by them, even when everyone else has turned their backs. That's a sign of real maturity.

Another sign of maturity is that one can be thankful when everything is going wrong. To have a sense of self-confidence and a sense of confidence in God when all of the chips are down is one of the most beautiful signs of maturity.

A person has reached manhood when he has a sense of obligation. His obligation is to serve his fellowman and his God. To accept responsibility for oneself and his acts and to have a sense of obligation to other people is the highest form of maturity that one can obtain.

PRAYER: May we put away childish things. *Amen.*

Kicking the Habit

And, as his custom was, he went into the
synagogue on the sabbath day.
Luke 4:16

Did you ever say, "I'd like to kick the habit"?
Sometimes we mean narcotics, sometimes we
mean booze, and sometimes we mean something else. I've heard it said that habits make a
man. I guess that's true, so good habits can
make a man or bad habits can make a man, or
should we say, unmake a man.

If our own choices can cause bad habits, then
right choices can cause good habits and help us
switch from bad to good habits.

Here are some suggestions that may give you
the strength you need to kick whatever habit
needs kicking. The first is good physical habits,
like getting enough sleep and the right food and
exercise, and relaxation. You have heard it said,
"All work and no play makes Jack a dull boy."
It's also true that all play and no work can raise
havoc. When we do just as we please with our
body and pay no attention to it, and forget that
the body is a gift from God, we are not exercis-
ing good physical habits.

It is important that we form habits that en-
able us to learn. I mean not only from our
school work but from our daily living experi-

ences. It is true, isn't it, that the best way to learn to drive a car is to drive one? And the best way to learn how to park a car is to park one? We learn from our experiences. But we must never let our experiences control us.

The same rule holds true when we speak of our religion. Here are some suggestions for forming good habits in religion. The first is to have a few moments every day when you just think about God and yourself or, as some people call it, private devotions. The second one is to do as the Bible Jesus did. "His custom was he went into the synagogue on the sabbath day." It is saying he went to church regularly to worship God.

Another very important religious habit is being helpful to someone else. Even when we don't have to.

When we are busy practicing good habits we seldom have time for bad ones.

PRAYER: May we be so busy with good and important habits that we have no time for anything else. *Amen.*

Run, Man, Run

Let us run with patience the race that
is set before us.
Heb. 12:1

Some people think of life as a race, or even a rat race. But that's not what I'm thinking about. Who ever wrote the book of Hebrews gave some suggestions that might help in running the race of life. The first is to look ahead. The words he used were "the race that is set before us." You can't win anything if you're going around in circles, or if you are always looking back.

Then he also told us to remember that we were not running alone. There are people all around us who dream dreams and have visions and have had experiences that can help us and encourage us. Getting help from other people when we really need it is not a sign of weakness, but a sign of strength. And it helps us in the race of life.

He also tells us we're to run with patience. Did you ever run across anybody who gave up right away when he tried something and it didn't quite work out the first time? Anybody who is going to win a race needs lots of guts to stick it out to the very end.

A forward look, a feeling of being a part of

the team, and patience can help when we take the most important step of all that this book in the Bible tells about. It's looking to Jesus as an example of the way in which the race is to be won.

PRAYER: Seems like we are always running, so let us run for a reason. *Amen.*

Shape Up, Man!

A new Commandment I give you: love one another. . . . If you have love for one another, then all will know you are my disciples.
John 13:34-35

If you live on an island all by yourself, just turn me off. You don't need to listen!

But if there are other people around and you are not alone, then how you live with other people, how you use whatever talents you have, takes first place.

We live by groups, some large, some small. You are not the only person at home, or school, or work or in the community—or even in jail. "Group relations" (or that's what the shrinks call it) becomes an important part of you.

You have heard of the Art of Painting, the Art of Singing. How about the Art of Living Together? It is an Art, and a real tough one to get with. How you get along with other people is one of life's biggest problems. How you make adjustments to what you find at home, or school, or wherever you are, sometimes tells what you are. If you do a "fast burn" every time you run up against a problem people will say, "He has a wild temper." That will be the way people will know you. It's what those shrinks call a character pattern. The character patterns we build now will be the ones we have later in life.

Makes sense, doesn't it, to let our life be influenced by what Jesus did as early as possible? What does Christ expect of us? How does he expect us to act? That's the question we need to ask ourselves when the way gets confused and dark and we feel boxed in.

PRAYER: Lord, show us how to be cool and honest with others. *Amen.*